Pamphlet Architecture 27

Tooling

Aranda/Lasch
Benjamin Aranda & Chris Lasch

foreword by Cecil Balmond
afterword by Sanford Kwinter
Princeton Architectural Press, New York

Published by
Princeton Architectural Press
37 East Seventh Street
New York, New York 10003

For a free catalog of books, call 1.800.722.6657.
Visit our web site at www.papress.com.

Printed and bound in Canada by Friesens
12 11   9 8 7

NATIONAL
ENDOWMENT
FOR THE ARTS

This project is supported in part by an award
from the National Endowment for the Arts.

Editor: Scott Tennent
Design: For Office Use Only

Special thanks to: Nettie Aljian, Dorothy Ball, Nicola Bednarek, Janet Behning,
Megan Carey, Penny (Yuen Pik) Chu, Russell Fernandez, Jan Haux, Clare Jacobson,
John King, Mark Lamster, Nancy Eklund Later, Linda Lee, Katharine Myers,
Lauren Nelson, Jennifer Thompson, Paul Wagner, Joseph Weston, and
Deb Wood of Princeton Architectural Press
—Kevin C. Lippert, publisher

Library of Congress Cataloging-in-Publication Data

Aranda, Benjamin.
Tooling / Aranda, Lasch.— 1st ed.
93 p. : chiefly ill. ; 22 cm. — (Pamphlet architecture ; 27)
ISBN 1-56898-547-9 (alk. paper)
1. Architectural design—Computer simulation. 2. Architecture—Computer-
aided design. I. Lasch, Chris. II. Title. III. Series.
NA2728.A58 2005
720'.1'13—dc22
                                                    2005024971

For Ali Malik, a dear and talented friend whose future life of bending and breaking architecture was cut short one sad summer day. Through him we know the responsibility of believing only in beginnings. *Benjamin Aranda*

And for my grandmother, Nancy Lasch Park, who earned a degree in architecture years before it was common for women to enter the field. I will always remember her spending many hours with me turning books and blocks into complex structures. She was my first and most loyal colleague. *Chris Lasch*

tool·ing *n.*

1. to form, work, or decorate with a tool
2. work or ornamentation done with tools, especially stamped or gilded designs on leather
3. the process of providing a factory with machinery in preparation for production
4. *slang*: To drive (a vehicle): *tooling the car at 80 mph*

Table of Contents

6   Foreword by Cecil Balmond
8   Introduction

10   Spiraling
22   Packing
32   Weaving
40   Blending
52   Cracking
62   Flocking
74   Tiling

92   Afterword by Sanford Kwinter

Benjamin Aranda and Chris Lasch produce an architecture that exposes the vitality of nested structures, their layering at various scales, and their simultaneity. It is as much about a process of self-organization as it is about the structures of pattern, which yield a cascade of intermeshed strategies for the derivation of form and texture. The method offers endless potential for the interpretation of program.

The nature of their search is algorithmic, the repeating dynamic that compiles and reveals a series of embedded orders. What we choose depends on materiality linked to scale. At the infinite, the proposals may hint at cosmic organization; at the micro and realm of compact densities, they intuit biological process. In between is a world of inventive speculation, where the imperative of a particular pattern drives the response toward a choice dictated purely by local features.

The fields traced out by these dancing movements open multiple pathways for the outcome of design. Using scripts as a tooling device, Aranda/Lasch offers a special looking glass into the labyrinths of potential space. Form and material arise from information strategies compounded along a time axis by algorithms. Instead of data being seen as indifferent, this approach offers data as alive and spontaneous, capable of self-ordering, embedded with vision if you know how to look. And Aranda/Lasch is doing just that in this book—they are showing us how to look.

Introduction
Benjamin Aranda & Chris Lasch

Imagine a few drops of water about to freeze. The endless variety of crystal shapes that emerge in that moment of crystallization became an obsession for one self-educated farmer from Vermont, Wilson Bentley, who spent a lifetime photographing snowflakes. For the forty-five years leading up to his death in 1931, through a painstaking process that involved brutal weather and fussy equipment, Bentley proved that no two snowflakes are alike by documenting 5,381 individual crystals falling behind his farmhouse. For him, the beautiful six-sided symmetry of every crystal was evidence of both the character of the cloud it came from, its altitude, electromagnetism, and temperature, as well as the rules inherent to the water molecule. Since science had not unraveled a working model of the atom yet, it was this last detail—the water molecule itself with its attractions and repulsions—that led Bentley to his exasperation in an article for *Technical World* in 1910: "What magic is there in the rule of six that compels the snowflake to conform so rigidly to its laws?" Beneath Bentley's exasperation is a yearning for the algorithmic; the rule of six is evidenced not only in the fact that all snowflakes are six-sided but right down to the molecules and the way they bond with each other, ultimately describing a molecular relationship between two hydrogen atoms and one oxygen atom. The rule of six unlocks his collection. It is a binding rule of transformation, an algorithm that connects the movement from "six" to "no two are alike."

If architecture is an extended process of formation, then before ideas coalesce into a definitive form there must exist some undifferentiated state free of any organization. The moment any sort of development is imposed onto this formless matter it begins to enter the realm of substance, organization, and material. *Tooling* is about what rules exist within this hypothetical "pre-material" state that influence its movement into the realm of the material. Like Bentley's snowflakes, the source of wonder behind one crystal is not the storm it came from but rather the elusive internal logic that remains resolute and unmoving through all crystals.

Tooling is broken down into seven algorithmic techniques: spiraling, packing, weaving, blending, cracking, flocking, and tiling. While each of these algorithms can be used to describe and simulate certain natural phenomena in the world—such as the way a spiraling rule can simulate a hurricane—this book is invested in turning these rules into logics for construction. The term *algorithm* simply means a series of steps. Today, as modeling, representation, and fabrication technologies shift from manual to automated processes, this issue of algorithm is pressing precisely because it confronts the design of procedures themselves. To illustrate this, all algorithmic techniques in *Tooling* are presented alongside 1) a recipe, 2) shapes made by that recipe, 3) a project that uses that recipe within an architectural context, and finally, 4) programmatic computer code (www.arandalasch.com/tooling) making these recipes available to the widest possible audience.

The recipe is vital to understand the basic steps in each algorithm. The maxim, "a problem well put is a problem half-solved," is no less true in the formulation of architectural techniques. In fact, only when these steps are clearly stated can they really become an algorithm, a powerful packaging of logic that allows this procedural thinking to migrate inside and through various syntaxes, including software. As evidence of this transmissible character, the tailor-made computer code for each of the recipes and sketches can be utilized within the major 3D modeling software platforms being used by architects today. The intent in sharing these algorithms is to encourage diversity, allowing others to import, model, and evolve more critical and insightful tools.

Algorithms also offer a non-technological implication in architecture. They break down the elusive and sometimes problematic phenomena of shape. Shapes are never unwilled figures. Deep within them is a struggle between the predilections of the architect and the inherent properties of the geometries encountered. The algorithm mediates these two, acting as a kind of solvent to liquefy them and create the potential for crystallization. *Tooling* traces the movement between this state of potential and manifest architecture. This movement, or movements, occurs in a dynamic space of interchange where the algorithms and the evolving diversity of figures that crystallize from them are in constant communication and formation with external pressures. The objective of *Tooling* is to both articulate this resonant field and show that one of the biggest challenges of algorithmic architecture lies in establishing very coherent, pre-material rules that can be used with mathematics and geometry to control this field. Once this field is defined as a flexible and open space, the job of designing begins.

Spiraling produces a shape unlike any other because it is seldom experienced as geometry, but rather as energy.

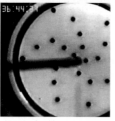

Whether stars, storm clouds, or petals of a flower, the spiral is only detectable by observing the things caught in its wake. Droplets of ferroliquid placed in a polarized solution (above) reveal that magnetic energy naturally distributes itself in a spiral manifestation. The form is also inherent in plant growth patterns, which allow the maximum number of petals to grow in the least amount of space. The spiral is not so much a shape as the evidence of a shape in formation.

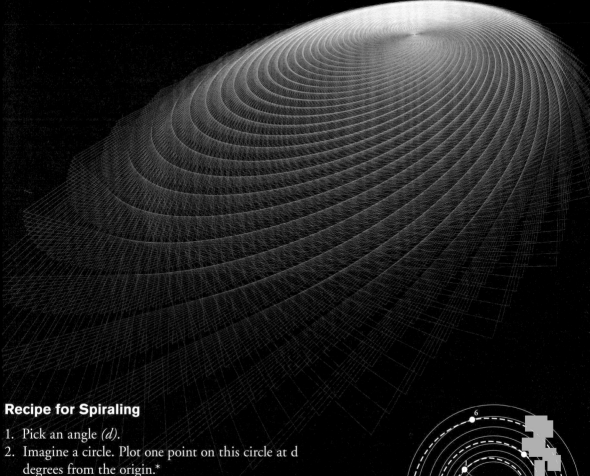

Recipe for Spiraling

1. Pick an angle *(d)*.
2. Imagine a circle. Plot one point on this circle at d degrees from the origin.*
3. Plot another point at *d* degrees from the last point on a concentric circle that is slightly bigger than the circle before it.
4. Repeat step 3.[†][‡]

d=137.5

---

* The coordinates of the *k*th point in a spiral lattice with divergence *d* and expansion parameter G are given by (Gk cos(kd), Gk sin(kd)).

† In a spiral lattice, the eye tends to connect nearest points into spirals. These spirals within the spiral are called parastichies. In plants, the number of these visible spirals are most often two successive elements of the Fibonacci sequence: one in which each number is the sum of the previous two.

‡ This model is typically used to describe *Phyllotaxis* (Greek *phyllo*, leaf + *taxis*, arrangement), a naturally occurring plant growth pattern that governs the arrangement of leaves, flower petals, pine cones, etc.

Experiments: Expanded Spiral Lattices

A series of points placed on concentric circles with a constant divergence angle between them is called a spiral lattice. This series of experiments uses a three-dimensional spiral lattice to project a structured envelope. The spiral lattice is promising as a formal proposition because there is a seemingly infinite number of spiral/sub-spiral configurations available from the finite of shared points plotted in the original lattice. Within any of these configurations it is easy to find multiple points of intersection to develop stability.

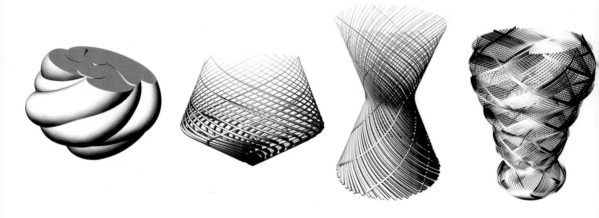

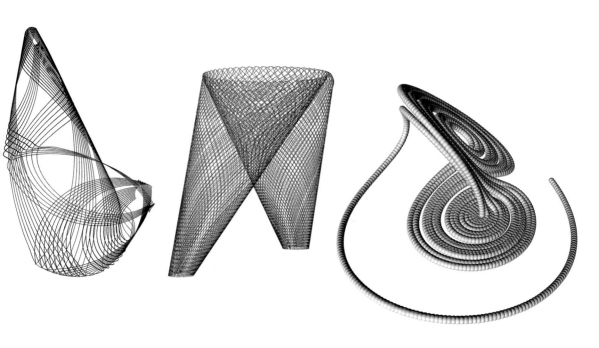

10-Mile Spiral

The spiral is an obsessive shape: it spreads out endlessly while it curls toward a center that it never finds. Las Vegas is an obsessive city: it too spreads out endlessly, as the fastest growing city in America and new business capital of the west; yet it also curls toward a center, the strip and its entertainment/gaming complexes. Our submission for the Las Vegas Sign Competition, 10-Mile Spiral, serves two civic purposes for Las Vegas. First, it acts as a massive traffic decongestion device, spreading out the bumper-to-bumper traffic occurring on weekends along I-15, the interstate corridor that eventually becomes the famous Las Vegas Strip. It does so by adding significant mileage to the highway in the form of a spiral. The second purpose is less infrastructural and more cultural: along the spiral you can play slots, roulette, get married, see a show, have your car washed, and ride through a tunnel of love, all without ever leaving your car. It is a compact Vegas, enjoyed at 55 miles per hour and topped off by a towering observation ramp offering views of the entire valley floor below.

Traffic

The problem of traffic congestion is one of perception. There is no way to stem the incoming and outgoing flow of vehicles to Las Vegas, but you can change how people perceive the time they spend on the road. As long as they keep moving they will not be bored or frustrated. With this in mind, the gateway serves to decongest existing traffic using a formula that states: while you will be going faster, you won't get there any sooner.

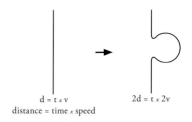

$$d = t \times v$$
distance = time $\times$ speed

$$2d = t \times 2v$$

Roulette

Car wash

Observation tower

Car slots

Original signage

Six circle lanes + six spiral lanes
= switching patterns for endless fun

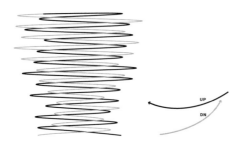

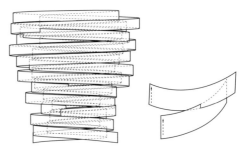

1. Dirty Spiral: an algorithm is employed to generate a helix whose radius varies randomly as it climbs and then falls back down to the valley floor.

2. Extrusion: a structural curb is extruded to fifteen feet to stiffen the ramp.

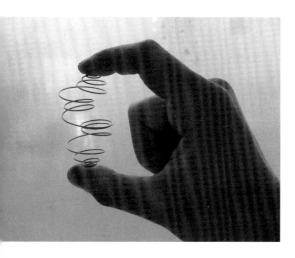

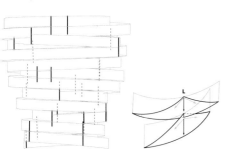

3. Load-transferring: intersection points between these strips are transfer points through which the structure's loads are channeled to the ground.

4. Beams: the structure is optimized to allow views out to the valley. Material is retained in the axial line of stress and removed where the curb is not doing any structural work.

Packing produces stability through adjacency.

Packing is a powerful organizational method in which an element's position in regard to its neighbors is determined by certain rules—not too close, no overlapping, etc. Packing encourages a sense of democracy where one element's inclusion implies either an understanding of every other element or possibly a readjustment of the entire population. Whether it is studied as self-organized structuring in cells or as a behavioral trope in crowds, packing can be observed as a collective and emergent sense of space—close, but not too close.

Recipe for Packing

1. Create a shape* of a random size.
2. Pick a random point.
3. a) If the shape is inside another shape, or overlaps another shape,† throw it away and go back to step 1.‡
   b) If not, place it. Go to step 1.

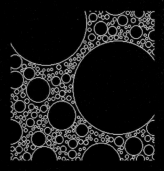

Osculatory packing (kissing method)

---

*   Spheres (circles) are naturally stable shapes. When packed together, they create a very strong construction, owing to the sphere's inherent stability and tendency for a collection of spheres to produce multiple points of tangency.

†   If the distance between the circles is less than the sum of their radii, then they overlap.

‡   Obviously, as more circles are placed, it gets harder and harder to place a new one. This is a brute force method.

Experiments: Three-Dimensional Slicing

Beyond serving as a dynamic system for producing flat organizations, packing also offers rich three-dimensional and material strategies when combined with other operations. Enter the cut: by slicing away at the packing studies, the algorithmic logic is released into new architectural possibilities.

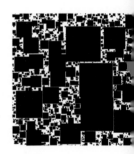

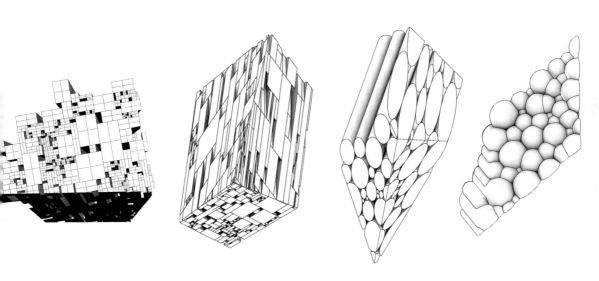

Log Cabin

Resurrecting an old log cabin that once occupied the site but had burned down in a fire is the starting point of this project. The construction of a log cabin is a serial operation of cutting trees and then stacking them. What would happen if this order were reversed—stack first, then cut? Through a material study it was surprising to see how much more the log could offer. By cutting after stacking, the tree's rings took center stage. Their structural potential through adjacency was released at the same time as their capacity to change shape, from circle to ellipse to bar. Structure and opacity can be controlled and reveal program, all through stacking and packing.

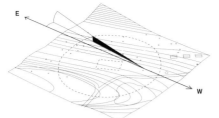

Circulation: use hill for ADA compliance

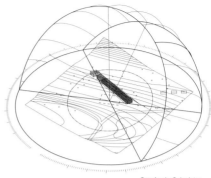

Sun Angle Calculator

Ground floor: shape and orient for views

Second floor: maximize solar gain, bedroom bar design
The hill bore the ramp and allowed for a two-story building. The second floor is conceived of as a "bedroom bar" which receives sun from the southern wall of windows and is isolated from the ground, making it an ideal thermal mass. All bedrooms and amenities are along the long east-west axis of the building in anticipation of passive solar heating.

Ground-floor plan

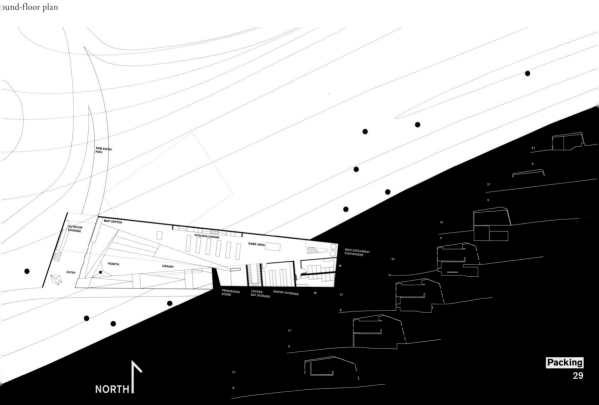

NORTH

Tiling

The north facade is left more opaque to minimize heat loss.
Self-similar patterns of seemingly infinite variety can be
produced by mirroring tiles and joining coded edges.

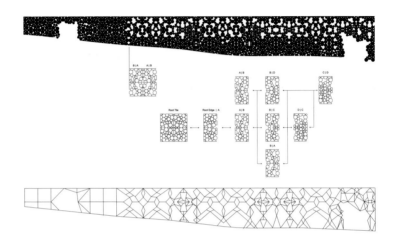

radient

e south-facing facade opens up toward the western edge of
building, where the common spaces are gathered to take
antage of the view.

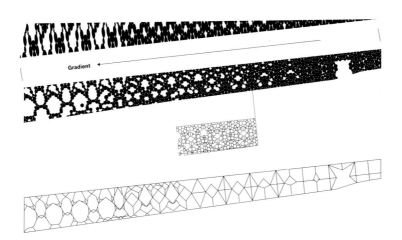

Gradient

Weaving produces strength by combining two weak systems in a reciprocal pattern.

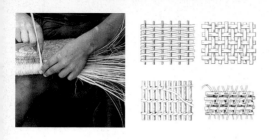

Weaving is the synthesis of two different systems, interlocking in order to give self-supporting form to their combined whole. Traditionally referred to as a "warp" and a "weft" pattern, neither could support themselves alone, but together they become strong. The endless variety of weaving seen in basket, net, rope, and textile design proves that procedural techniques and cultural practices are not mutually exclusive. Most surprising about a woven construction is that it is actually harder to unravel than to weave in the first place.

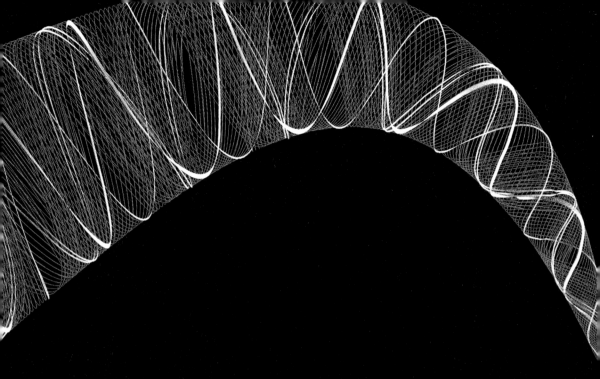

Recipe for Weaving

1. Start drawing a sin curve: a line that goes around a circle at a steady rate, spread out over time.*
2. Loop the curve by adding a term—a mathematical function, like cos ( )—that speeds up and slows down the line as it goes around the circle.†‡
3. Add more terms to create more loops, overlaps, and squiggles.
4. Mirror the curve for a denser, interlocking figure.§

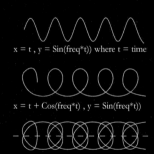

$x = t$, $y = \text{Sin}(\text{freq}^*t)$) where t = time

$x = t + \text{Cos}(\text{freq}^*t)$, $y = \text{Sin}(\text{freq}^*t)$

The curve above, mirrored around the X-axis:
$x = t + \text{Cos}(\text{freq}^*t)$, $y = \text{Sin}(\text{freq}^*t)$ &:
$x = t + \text{Cos}(\text{freq}^*t)$, $y = -(\text{Sin}(\text{freq}^*t))$

----

* The components of the equation are scale, frequency, and amplitude. These mathematical attributes replace the traditional knotmaking procedures of translation, turning, and reflection. Either one of these sets of attributes can produce an endless variety of forms that are traceable back to simple rules.

† Adding a cos ( ) term in the x portion of the equation affects the horizontal expansion of the points that make up the curve. The x term pushes or pulls these points along the "time" line (t) until the curve begins to loop back on itself.

‡ Adding a z term gives a three-dimensional aspect to the curve.

§ Many traditional weaving patterns make use of symmetry because it provides guaranteed points of overlap that help to structure the weave.

Experiments: Crossing Patterns

These sketches use a parametric equation to organize a series of sine and cosine curves in space. The weave is a crossing pattern, a "soft" structure of loops and knots wherein the shape of the construction is determined less by the properties of the materials themselves than by the pattern through which two sets of materials interact.

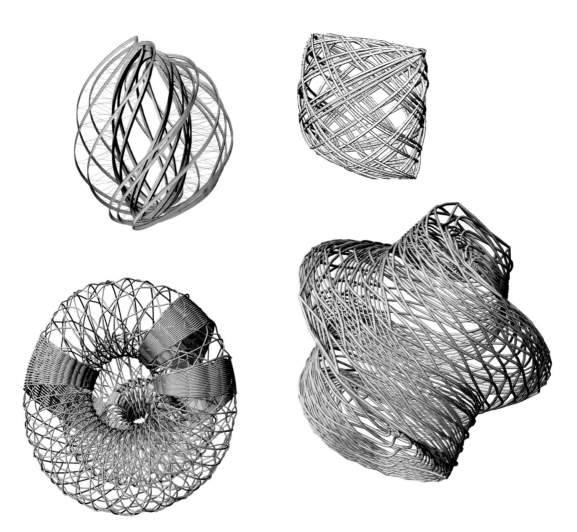

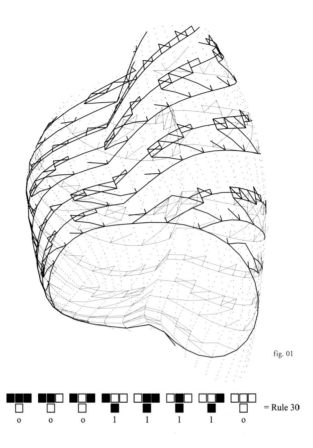

fig. 01

= Rule 30

o   o   o   1   1   1   1   o

Computational Basketry

Weaving is a binary process. Over/under and warp/weft are binary, or mutually exclusive states that structure a weave much in the same way that 1/0 and on/off structure a digital file. This project aims to explore this shared foundation through an experimental collaboration with Terrol Dew Johnson, an acclaimed Native American basketweaver. This initial set of experiments employs a cellular automata (CA) program to produce a weave accross a shape that is defined by a distribution of points, or nodes. The CA algorithm produces a rule-set based on binary values that structure the decision-making process for each node in the pattern. CA procedures can produce incredibly intricate and complex weaves because the algorithm is automatically feeding information back to itself to make the next decision. This causes the weave to adapt and change as it travels over its surface. In fig. 01 each node looks at the state of the three nodes that preceded it in the weave. The rule-set determines which states will prompt a new connection (shown above in black) and which will not. There may be dead ends, but every weave is continous.

Rule 45 single seed

Rule 60 single seed

Rule 110 random seed

Rule 110 random seed

Rule 60 single seed

Blending is a fundamental technique in the act of negotiation.

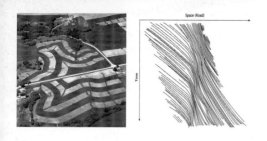

Blending holds that given any two original states—such as speed, time, shape, or contour—an infinite number of substates are available to establish a connection between them. The cultivation of land for agriculture displays a blended pattern negotiating shape and contour; the mapping of traffic congestion over time shows that speeds are blended through critical thresholds on the road. Their underlying mathematical logic is encouraging because it dictates that a commonality between any two states can be easily determined.

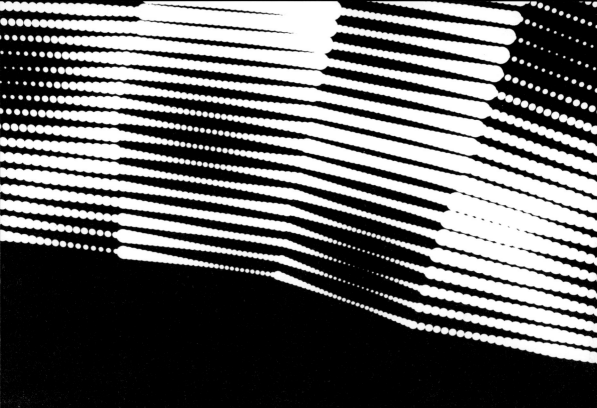

Recipe for Blending

1. Pick two shapes, a beginning state and an ending state.[*]
2. Break the shapes down into an equal number of constituent points[†] in space.
3. Divide up the space between the two shapes in an interesting way.[‡]
4. Interpolate between a point on one shape and the corresponding point on the other shape by taking the distance between them and multiplying by the current ratio;[§] each division is a ratio of the whole (1/4, 1/3, 1/2, etc.) Repeat for each point, by each division.

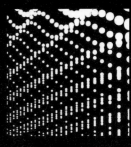

---

[*] Copying is a subset of blending, it is the morphing of objects without changing its state.

[†] In this instance, points are the constituent parts of our quality: shape. The same principle holds for blending colors (rgb), positions (x, y), scale (%), or any other attribute.

[‡] This is really the heart of the algorithm. It determines the smoothness of the transition between states and also the "curve" of the change—its frequency profile. The space can be divided into equal parts, or a function can be applied to adjust that ratio. An exponential function (n2) makes the space between each division get progressively bigger while a root function (√n) will make the divisions progressively smaller.

[§] This creates a field of points between the two initial shapes that can be used to modify the initial geometry or can be taken as a framework with which to weave an entirely new system into the first one.

Experiments: Aggregate Surfaces

These experiments were produced by modifying and extending the blending algorithm and its variables, pursuing an interest in the description of shapes in space and the relationships between them. Since it is necessary to first break a shape down in order to fully understand its qualities, it is an investigation into decomposition, not as a destructive act, but a creative one.

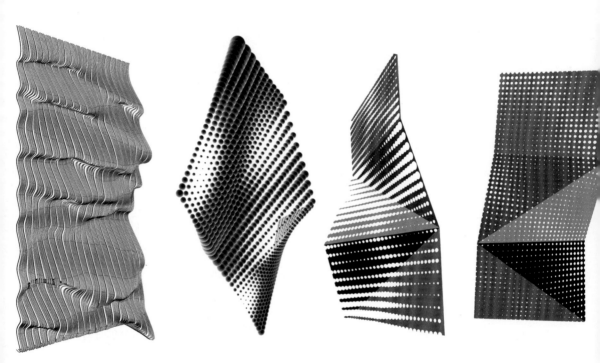

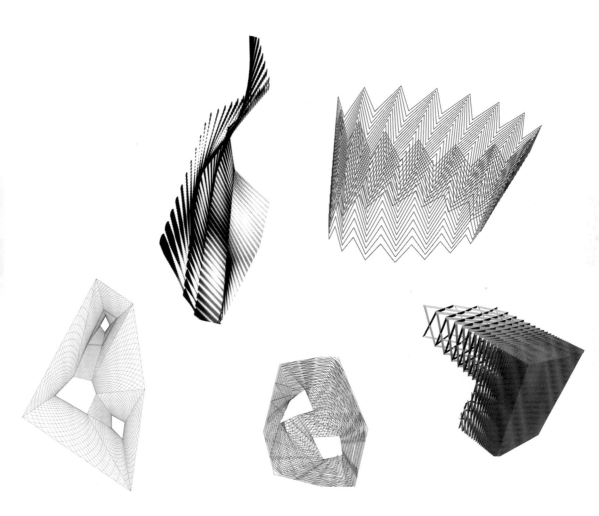

Camouflage View

Camouflage is the art of concealment, disguising an object in plain sight. As part of the International Garden Festival at the Reford Gardens in Mont-Joli, Quebec, Canada, *Camouflage View* almost conceals a spectacular panorama of the St. Lawrence River by confusing foreground and background, a common strategy in animal camouflage. Utilizing a zebra effect, the installation is itself camouflaged, challenging the viewers to discover it as well as the oncoming vista amidst reflections of the foregrounding green. By looking carefully at the construction, they are looking carefully at the environment around them.

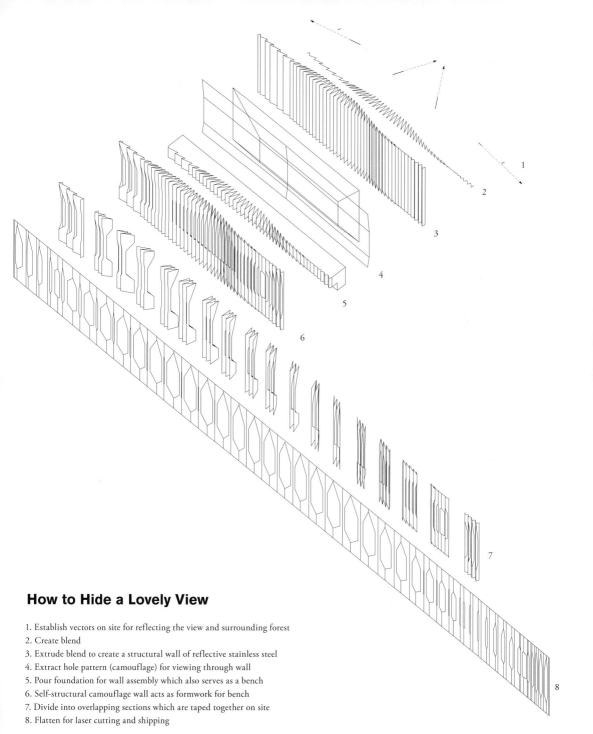

How to Hide a Lovely View

1. Establish vectors on site for reflecting the view and surrounding forest
2. Create blend
3. Extrude blend to create a structural wall of reflective stainless steel
4. Extract hole pattern (camouflage) for viewing through wall
5. Pour foundation for wall assembly which also serves as a bench
6. Self-structural camouflage wall acts as formwork for bench
7. Divide into overlapping sections which are taped together on site
8. Flatten for laser cutting and shipping

Following the rule of self-similarity, `cracking` gives a sense of the larger whole.

By recalling its source shape recursively, cracking generates
a geometry of self-similarity. For instance, a river delta has
variously scaled "triangles" that are each "cracked" by the
iterative and aggregate process of fluvial erosion. The crack
patterns in dry mud or paint show a similar recursion of
shapes in at least two visible scales. Whether it is the dynamics
of water channeling through sediment to produce a delta or
heat and dryness causing paint to peel, cracking is a distinct
action performed through materials.

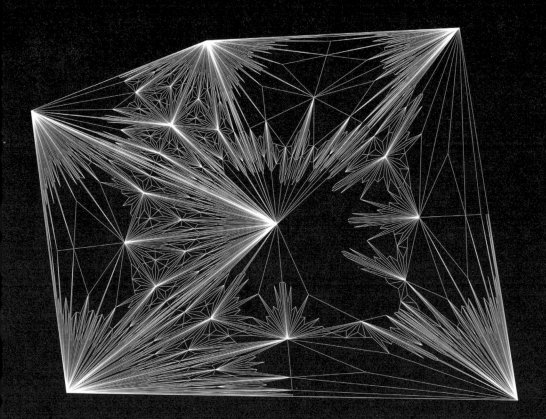

Recipe for Cracking

1. Choose a shape to be cracked.
2. Find its centroid.
3. Create subsidiary shapes by connecting the centroid to each end of one edge of the parent shape.
4. Repeat steps 2 and 3 for each new shape.*†
5. Continue until a limit is reached. Choose an iteration of the algorithm whose subsidiary shapes will be left whole.‡

---

* This algorithm produces a construction in which each edge is shared by exactly two shapes and each edge is continuous—connected to an edge which is connected to an edge, and so on—no matter how dense the mesh becomes.

† If one were to localize the cracking—crack more in one part of the structure than another—one could create patches made up of a higher number of shorter members.

‡ Each iteration contains an exponentially greater number of shapes than the one before it. Each iteration takes an exponentially longer time to process.

Experiments: Recursive Sketches

The cracking algorithm used in these sketches is one that takes a shape and divides it according to a value set by the user. In each instance, the shape is being recurred to another set of self-similar shapes. Recurring is about a return to origins within each new crack: the subdivision expresses something unique about the initial state from which it began. It is an embedded logic impossible to escape and fascinating to watch proliferate.

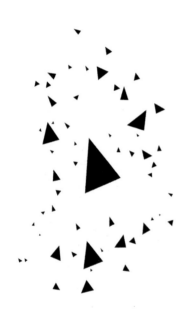  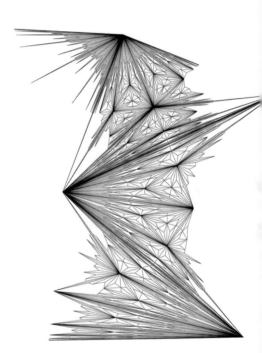

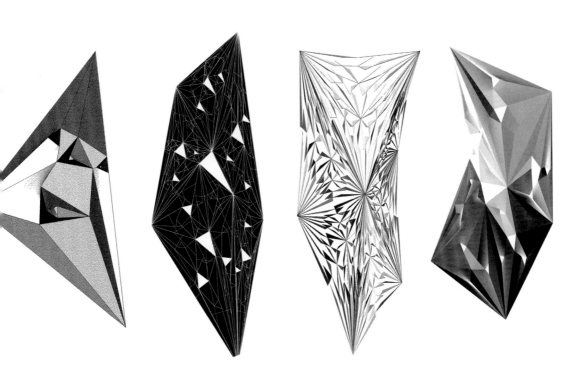

Delta, a River Museum

The Busan River Ecology Museum sits at the edge of a tidal river with the stated program of creating a learning environment about the river itself. A building on a river is also part of the river and thereby subject to its forces of erosion and formation. This proposal imagines the building's own formation in the same way a river delta is formed—through iterative aggregation and removal. The cracking procedure allows for both an organization and distribution of tidal movements that make the building behave like a mouth of a river, with branching waterways and triangular alluvial deposits acting as repositories for the museum program.

5

4

3

2

1

Sections

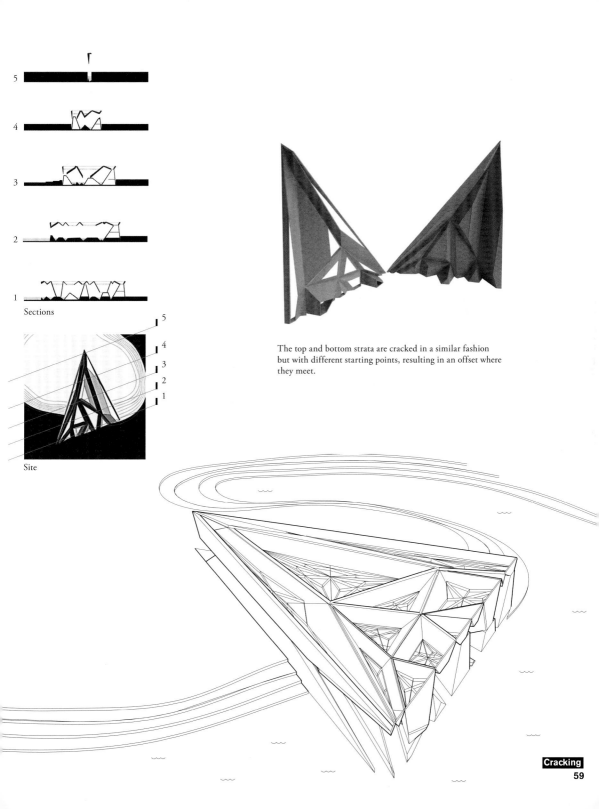

5
4
3
2
1

Site

The top and bottom strata are cracked in a similar fashion but with different starting points, resulting in an offset where they meet.

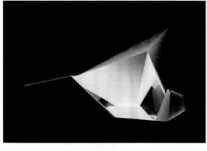

Nighttime view toward entrance

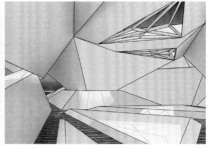

Interior

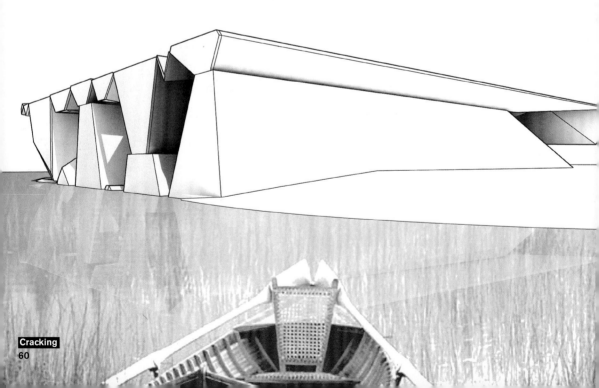

elta Formation

of
nation

und
nation

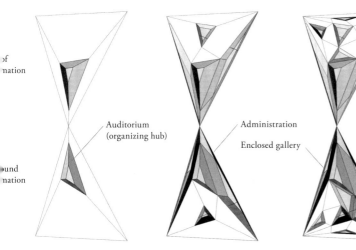
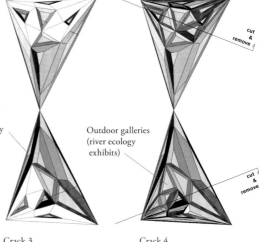

Auditorium
(organizing hub)

Administration

Enclosed gallery

Outdoor galleries
(river ecology
exhibits)

cut
&
remove

cut
&
remove

Crack 1
Major programmatic divisions

Crack 2
Major structural extrusions

Crack 3
Minor structural webbing

Crack 4
Tertiary structural reinforcement

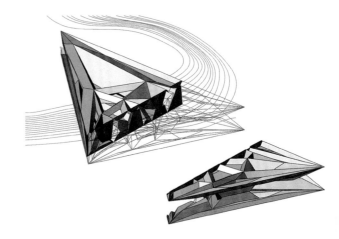

Cut & Remove
Cracking always tends toward vertices,
and since a delta has only one mouth,
the elimination of the other two
vertices was necessary.

Flocking finds order through entropy.

There is no better way to illustrate how complexity can erupt from many local interacting decisions than flocking. The individual elements might be plants and animals in an ecosystem, vehicles in traffic, or people in crowds. If one considers the city a dynamic in which systems of flow—such as traffic, circulation of goods, or crowd behavior—can be applied to any urban transformation, then flocking provides a vital model of complex coordination that describes these material shifts.

Recipe for Flocking

1. For each agent,* for each increment of time:
   a) Avoid crowding local flockmates. Steer to keep a
      minimum distance between each agent and the ones
      around it.†
   b) Align towards the average heading of local flockmates.
   c) Cohere to the flock, move toward the center mass‡ of
      local flockmates.

a

b

---

* Craig Reynolds first compiled the classic flocking algorithm in 1986 in a project
  simulating the way that birds and other flocking, herding, and schooling animals
  behave. He called his computer-simulated agents Boids—a contraction of birds and
  droids. Flocking continues to be an evocative example of emergence, where complex
  global behavior can arise from the interaction of simple local rules.

† In flocking models, a boid reacts only to flockmates within a certain neighborhood
  around itself; there is no global steering intelligence. The neighborhood is defined
  by a distance from the center of the boid and an angle around it, measured from its
  direction of travel.

‡ The "center mass" is the average position of all the agents.

c

Experiments: Traffic Flocks

Of all modes of human transportation, vehicular traffic is most poised with the potential to flock. The word "traffic" is usually taken to mean "too many cars," but it can also imply the simple flow of cars along a roadway. The congestion that it commonly describes is but one side of the equilibrium, that of stagnation. However, with adjustments to the roadway (no lanes) and vehicular technology (collision aversion), traffic jams can be reversed into productive entities; flocks that yield formations of order tethering at the edge of control. Studies in traffic flocking point toward massive-scaled, first-come/first-serve organizations where desires for moving, shopping, and playing merge on a single, self-organized plane of mutual cooperation.

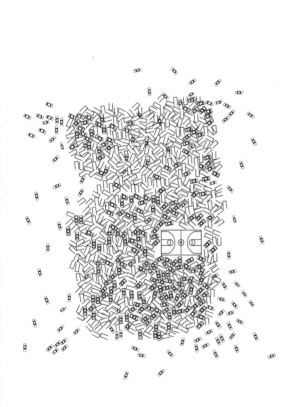

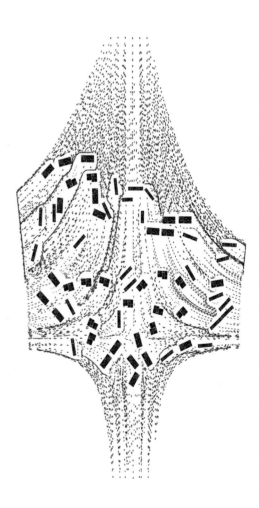

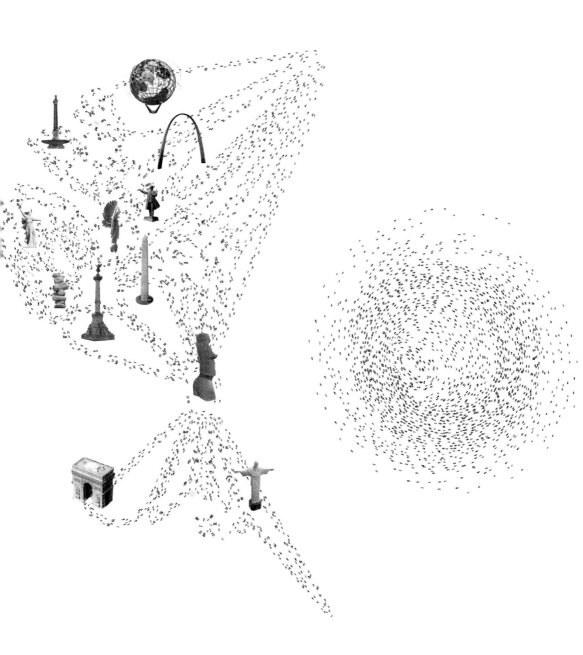

The Brooklyn Pigeon Project

The Brooklyn Pigeon Project is an experiment in developing a satellite that records the city as seen by a flock of birds. Using trained pigeons and working with seasoned bird flyers, the project team equips pigeons that fly in regular spiral patterns over swatches of Brooklyn with wireless video cameras and microphones. Harnessed to these custom cameras and small battery packs, the birds become satellites carrying "earth-sensing" equipment that feeds images and sounds of the city back to a ground location. Their flight paths capture unconventional portraits both of the city below and of flock motions. This unique way to see Brooklyn contrasts directly with the way the city is increasingly recorded and represented today. The advent of geographic information technologies and the rise of network protocols have placed virtually all urban imaging and remote sensing systems "on the grid." Using a flock of birds as one component of an imaging apparatus, this project attempts to confront the limits of this grid by creating an equally rich disclosure of the city: seeing the city as a flock would.

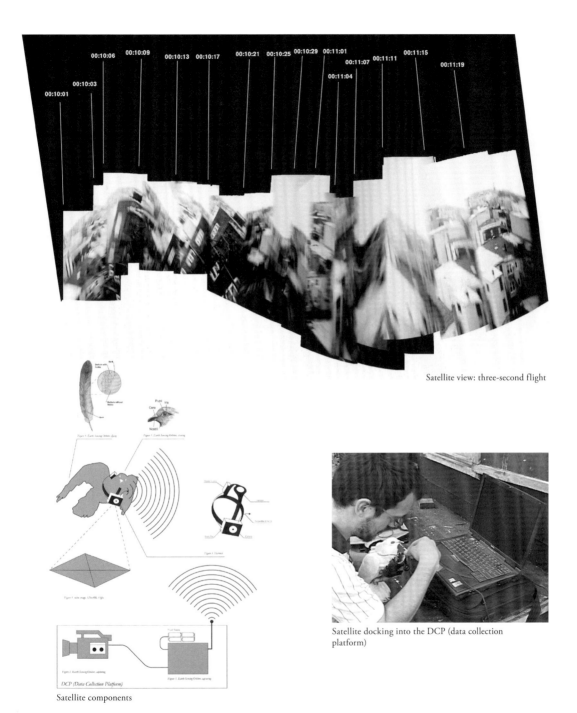

00:10:01 00:10:03 00:10:06 00:10:09 00:10:13 00:10:17 00:10:21 00:10:25 00:10:29 00:11:01 00:11:04 00:11:07 00:11:11 00:11:15 00:11:19

Satellite view: three-second flight

Satellite docking into the DCP (data collection platform)

Satellite components

Stills from sortie 3, May 2003

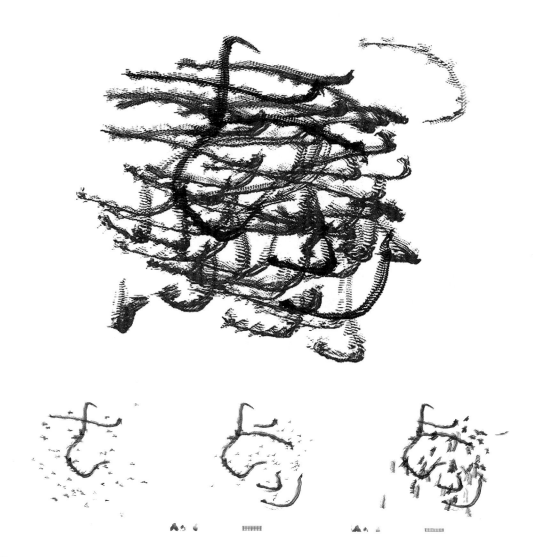

eeling

e tracings of bird movements within a flock confirms that distinct and sometimes
osed movements are nestled in the overall envelope. The path of a bird on one side
the flock is different from a bird on another side. Most surprising are the pronounced
erences; instead of slight variations, trajectories are tangled and intersecting. This
iation proves that the rule of separation was stronger than that of cohesion. So strong,
act, that some birds almost seem to be peeling away from the body of the flock. The
nomenon of peeling is important to understanding the flock's dynamic. It describes
oment of partial disintegration, a tear in a moving fabric. Birds make quick, local
isions based on what nearby birds are doing. As logic goes, if a bird follows another, it
st necessarily peel away from yet another.

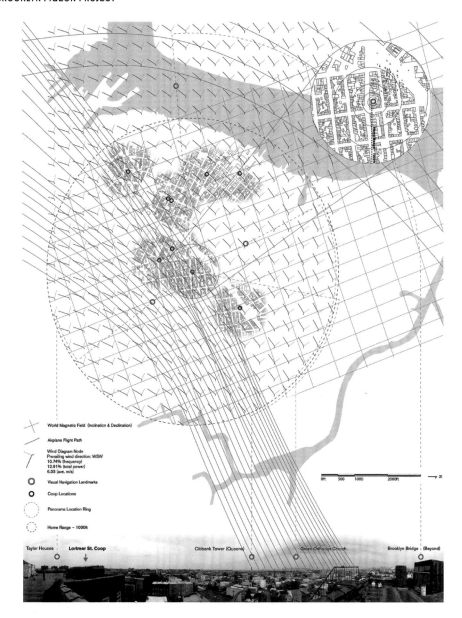

World Magnetic Field (Inclination & Declination)

Airplane Flight Path

Wind Diagram Node
Prevailing wind direction: WSW
10.74% (frequency)
12.91% (total power)
6.33 (ave. m/s)

Visual Navigation Landmarks

Coop Locations

Panorama Location Ring

Home Range ~ 1000ft

Taylor Houses | Lorimer St. Coop | Citibank Tower (Queens) | Greek Orthodox Church | Brooklyn Bridge | (Beyond)

0ft   500   1000   2000ft

Pigeon Atmospheres

Pigeons are sensitive to a variety of environmental stimuli. In addition to orienting themselves by the sun and visible landmarks, they respond to sound, smells carried on the prevailing winds, and even sense the Earth's magnetic field. This is a map of the pigeon atmosphere over Williamsburg, Brooklyn, NY. It depicts the field of play for the neighborhood's pigeon flyers.

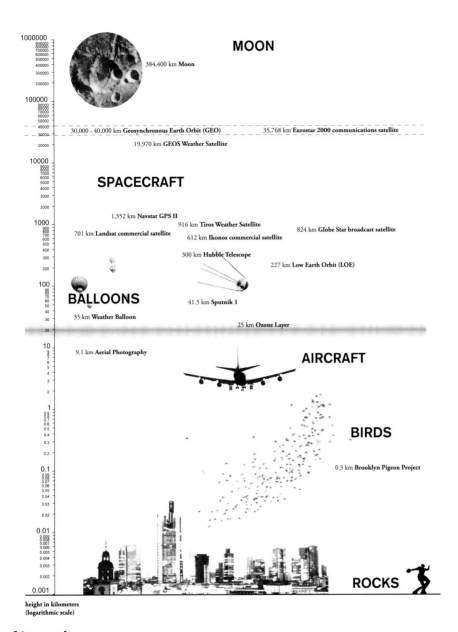

height in kilometers
(logarithmic scale)

atellite Atmospheres

any altitude, the ability to exploit gravity's pull is the defining character of a satellite.
wton described a satellite as anything projected horizontally over the surface of the
rth. This may include a rock or any aviary, celestial, or mechanical body.

Tiling assembles a patterned tectonic.

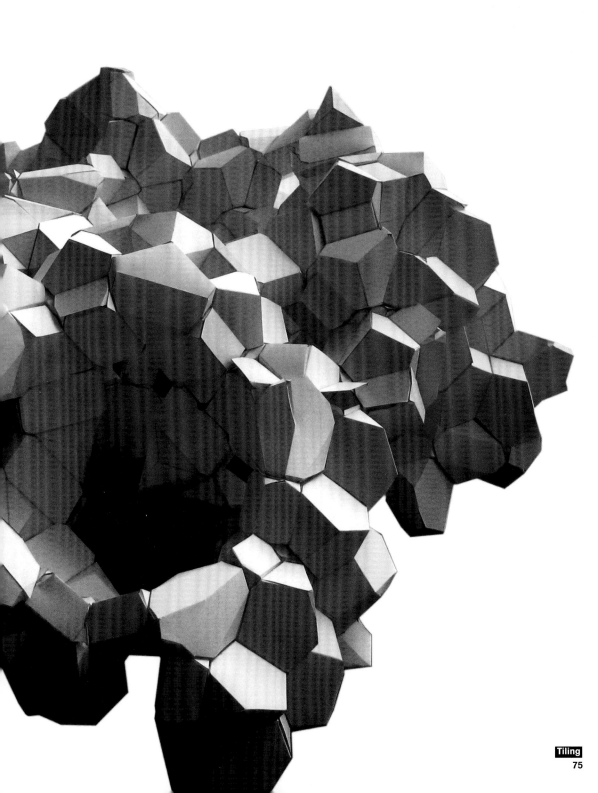

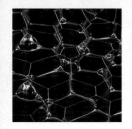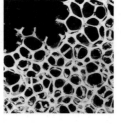

Along with repetition and modularity, the characteristic of tiling that provides such inspiration to tectonics is the issue of adjacency. The minimal enclosure system of bubbles and cells show that tiling need not be a flat system. Rather, its thickness in three dimensions organizes a constructive expansion toward infinity in all directions without any gaps.

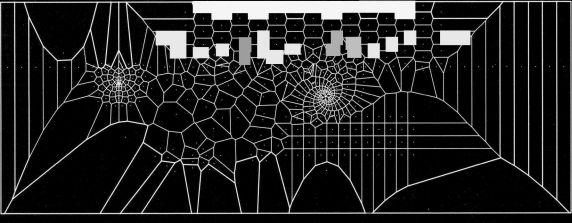

Recipe for Tiling

1. Take a set of points.
2. Construct a bisector between one point and all the others.*
3. The voronoi† cell is bounded by the intersection of these bisectors.‡
4. Repeat for each point in the set.

_____

* The bisector is halfway between two points at an angle perpendicular to a line that would connect the two points.

† Voronoi diagrams are of a class of patterns called Dirichlet tessellations, irregular tessellations of the plane that occur spontaneously in nature at every scale and are used in the study of many fields including biology, anthropoltogy, computer science, marketing, and the growth of crystalline structures—problems that involve opportunistic occupancy of space.

‡ Any intersection found to be on the far side of a bisecting line is ignored.

1.

2.

3.

Experiments: Subdividing Space

Each of these experiments involves the creation of a Voronoi tiling from a
point set. They result in cellular patterns where each cell contains all of the
space that is closer to its point than to any other point. They form a collection
of shapes that can look like squares, honeycombs, crystals, or boulders—the
nesting of other orders within a patterned, minimal enclosure system.

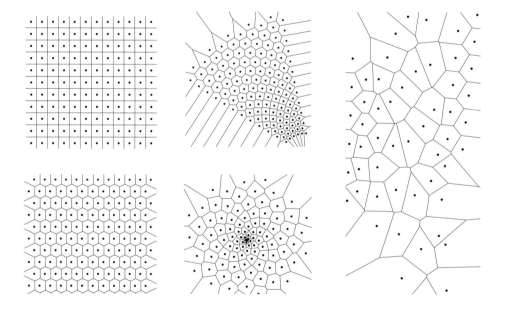

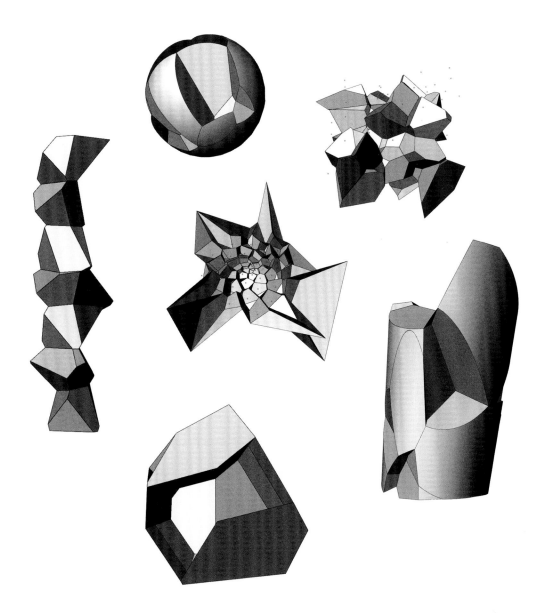

Grotto *in collaboration with Daniel Bosia, Arup AGU*

The grotto is an artificial structure or excavation in a garden made to resemble a cave. It is always elaborately artificial, absurdly fake. Against this backdrop of theatricality, forbidden pleasures can occur: hidden and discovered, stolen and intimate. The grotto found its heyday in eighteenth-century English gardens, providing a dark and erotic narrative to the landscape gardener's palette. This proposal for a temporary summer pavilion takes advantage of the grotto's essential feature: there is something to discover within, and that something is often wet.

Modular Boulders

Since the structural unit of a grotto is the boulder, the challenge of the project was to develop a set of modular boulders that combine in a way that defies a conventional sense of order. The solution uses a combination of algorithms, based on voronoi geometries, that transfer modularity from a Danzer tiling technique (developed at Arup AGU) to a final set of four faceted boulders. These four boulders fit together in a variety of ways. The result is a wildly ordered three-dimensional pattern that never repeats the same way twice.

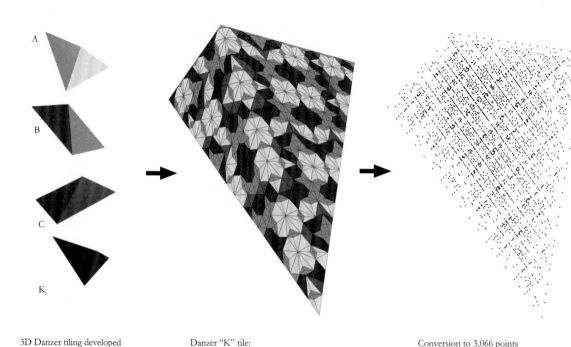

A

B

C

K

3D Danzer tiling developed
at Arup AGU

Danzer "K" tile:
seven generations:
11,382 triangles (tetrahedrals)

Conversion to 3,066 points

he Danzer tiling was carried out to the seventh generation to produce a
:rahedral packing. But while triangles make great patterns, a triangle is not
oulder. In order to create boulders (the structural unit of the grotto), it was
cessary to strip the tetrahedral packing down to its verticies. This revealed a
·int field from which we could derive a boulder tiling. The result resembled
oulder mess that, on closer inspection, was actually highly structured and
mposed of only four unit-types—the harmonies and modularity of the Danzer
ing translated.

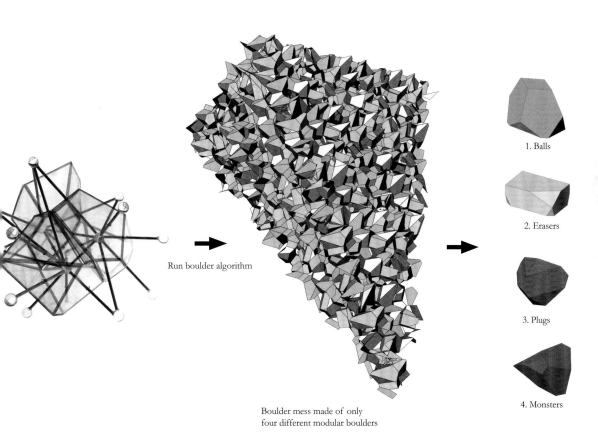

Run boulder algorithm

Boulder mess made of only
four different modular boulders

1. Balls

2. Erasers

3. Plugs

4. Monsters

Arching

Each of the four boulders behaves in its own way. Plug
and Eraser boulders form a very stable ring configuration
and became the basic structural unit of the project.
These rings connect together to form arches and vaults.
Since most of the spaces in the project would be made
from purely compressive structures, a majority of the EPS
foam boulders could simply be glued together. Only a
few of the larger vaults, where rings are daisy-chained
together, require any steel reinforcement.

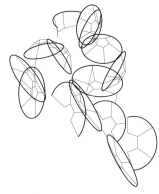

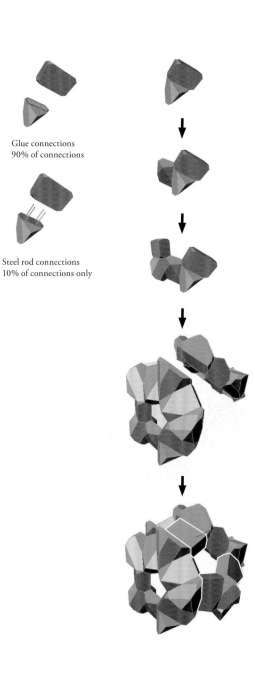

Glue connections
90% of connections

Steel rod connections
10% of connections only

Excavation

By excavating space out of this non-repetitive three-
dimensional pattern, a grotto space is formed and
adjusted to the program.

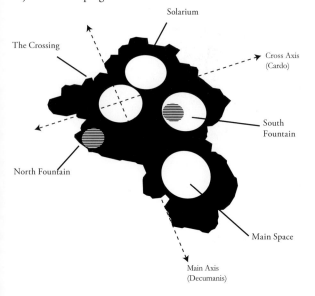

Solarium

The Crossing

Cross Axis
(Cardo)

South
Fountain

North Fountain

Main Space

Main Axis
(Decumanis)

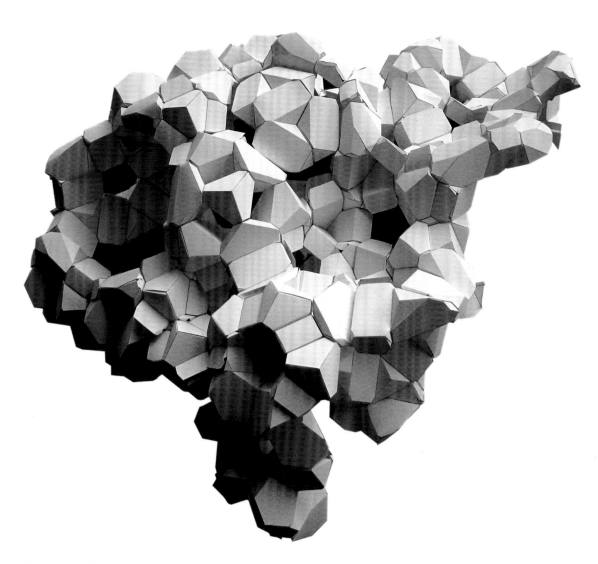

Folded paper model of excavated grotto

Jules-Joseph Lefebvre
Mary Magdalene in the Grotto

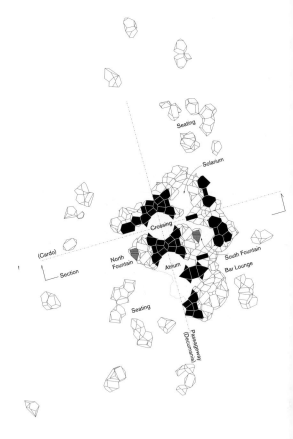

Plan 0'-0"

Plan 8'-0"

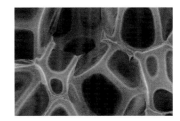

Microscopic view, EPS foam

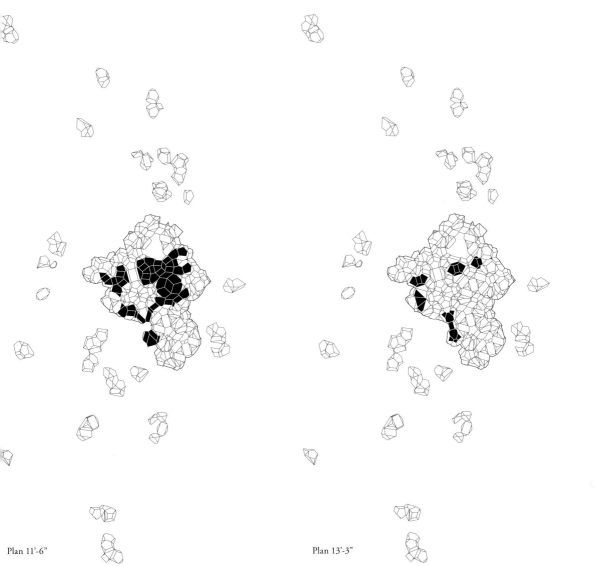

Plan 11'-6"

Plan 13'-3"

South fountain

Section through fountains   S. fountain   Passageway   N. fountain

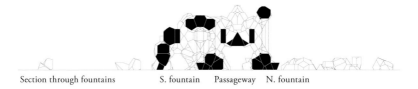

Section through passageway

…th fountain

"Within, fresh water and seats in the living rock, the home of the nymphs."
—Virgil, *The Aeneid*

Seven

Alfred North Whitehead once said that the day a connection was forged in the human mind between a group of seven fishes in a river and a group of seven days, a landmark advance was achieved in the history of thought. The thing referred to as "seven"—a thing not *per se* findable anywhere in nature outside of the human mind, and not distinguishable from the concrete bodies through which it is expressed—was an abstraction that we nonetheless soon came to think of as reality itself, and we began to live there.

The energy stored in a group of fish can be distributed across an expanse of time in a way that optimizes expenditure, supply, and demand. No fish, or man, ever saw or knew anything of a seven, but once the principle was imagined, it worked. And not once, but always.

Even today we do not know if numbers are real. (Some of our numbers are called Real, but that only underscores the fact that some obviously are not, a fact which alone does not seem to diminish either their usefulness or our interest in them.) Whitehead was also quick to point out that for the most part we modern people know little of real space, since numbers have been used for centuries to create the idea of location out of nothing (a mere directory of addresses), and that we have lost the sense of what the myriad processes that produce and populate space might be. These processes are incessant; they are said to be nature itself.

One of the great advances in thought in our own era happened when a connection was formed between the processes of nature and the world of forms. Certainly Aristotle was not the first to think about this relationship, but he did not achieve the same breakthrough that the man who discovered seven had done that day when he put an end to his episodic hunger. (Guided more by logic than by intuition or empirical method, Aristotle believed that eggs harbored homunculi and that men had more teeth and ribs than women.) The groundbreaking moment can be said to have come first with Goethe, who had the capacity to see the active genetic processes that operate inside of forms and which he called "Ur-forms." Urforms were not at all "originary" forms as is frequently thought, but rather the *foundational programs* that families of forms share with one another and which determine both their visible kinships and their irreducible differences. The Urform does not exist in the world like a dog or a fish or a plant, but more like a seven—or, shall we say, like a seven with a twist. You don't find it in the forest (even though that is where you go to look for it); you find it deep in the crosstalk of forms.

The idea of the Urform was never properly understood and furthermore became trapped in reductionist prejudices against Romantic philosophy. It was revived arguably by the General Systems Theory of the 1920s, which reviewed the known data on biogenesis and found it wanting. By the late 1930s, the phenomena denoted by what Goethe called Urforms received a new name and status through the research of Alonso Church and Alan Turing. They saw that numbers could be *automated* within functions—this was the twist—in order to express precisely and in a controlled environment what Goethe could only hope to glimpse within the wildness of nature. Church and Turing invented the modern performing *algorithm*. (They could only imagine these as machines, but since no such machines existed, they effectively invented them: computers.)

Design has tried to get hold of the immense performative power of algorithms for almost a decade. Few designers have succeeded in breaking with the misleading precedent of "simple location," the doctrine that sees geometry and space as describable by relatives of "seven," as a compound determination of fixed places.

The rule drives the algorithm and the rule is not a number. The rule is a pressure that is always limited by another rule. Rules do not make forms—the limitations that rules impose on one another do. (This phenomenon leads to what is known in computational science as "poisedness.")

If one looks well and deeply at the seven verbs of facture of Aranda/Lasch— spiral, pack, weave, blend, crack, flock, and tile—one might see the foundations of a true language where, just as in nature, the need for nouns and their false concreteness has proven to be a long and hilarious mistake. At the very least Aranda/Lasch seems to have grasped something that has eluded many others: that one needs cranes not only to create edifices, but also to build the larger cranes without which one cannot create the greater and most demanding edifices. To put it more directly: design must not focus uniquely on first order regulatory processes but must target the second order controls that regulate the regulatory processes themselves. The genius of nature and design meet precisely here. Why did it take so long?

New York City, September 18, 2005

Notes on *Tooling*

All the *Tooling* experiments were constructed through simple steps, repeated over and over until something of substance was revealed. These steps are usually straightforward geometric transformations—short sets of rules that we develop—sometimes to build a custom tool that had not yet existed, but more often to better understand the forms we wish to make. Tapping the number-crunching power of the computer opens up new design possibilities and gives us the capacity to grow and proliferate structures that we otherwise could not, but probably more important is deciding when to curb their growth, cut their shape, or stop using them altogether. We are cataloging all the code for users who wish to propagate them for their own purposes in the same way that we borrowed, edited, and repurposed code that was made available to us.

Scripts from tooling experiments are available at
www.arandalasch.com/tooling

Image Sources
p38: Terrol Dew Johnson, *Vase Basket*. Courtesy of the artist.
p38: Rule 30 diagram from Stephen Wolfram, *A New Kind of Science* (Champaign, IL: Wolfram Media, 2002), 53.
p48-49: Photograph by Louise Tanguay, Jardins de Métis/Reford Gardens.
p84: Antoine Joseph Dezallier D'Argenville, *Arboreal Stone and Florentine Stones*, 1755. Photo: Bibliotheque Nationale. From Jurgis Baltrusaitis, *Aberrations* (Cambridge, Mass.: MIT Press, 1989), 92.

Project Credits:
10-Mile Spiral: Benjamin Aranda, Chris Lasch. First Place, Vegas Sign Competition hosted by the Contemporary Arts Collective & Desert Space, 2004. Special thanks to Joshua Abbey.
Log Cabin: Benjamin Aranda, Chris Lasch, Todd Wilcox. Finalist, Palisade Glacier Mountain Hut Competition hosted by the Weiner Family Fund & The U.S. Park Service, 2003.
Computational Basketry: Benjamin Aranda and Chris Lasch in collaboration with Terrol Dew Johnson. Special thanks to Elizabeth Slocum, Bill Taylor, Aaron Dorf, Chrles Overy of LGM, Sean Hanna and the Smart Geometry Group. Supported by ACAIDA Fabrication Conference 2005 and the New York State Council for the Arts Independent Project Grant, 2005.
Camouflage View: Benjamin Aranda, Chris Lasch, Ajay Manthripragada. Competition winner, 2005 International Garden Festival Reford Gardens/Jardins de Métis. Special thanks to Lesley Johnstone, Yvan Maltais, and Alexander Reford.
Delta Museum: Benjamin Aranda, Chris Lasch. Competition entry, 2004 (unsubmitted). Thanks to Jeff Goldenson and Ajay Manthripragada.
Brooklyn Pigeon Project: Benjamin Aranda, Chris Lasch. Thanks to Arthur Diaz, Chris Hansen, Jose Rivera, Anthony Camera, Thomas Soehl. Supported by the New York State Council for the Arts Film and New Media Production Grant.
Grotto: Aranda/Lasch in collaboration with Daniel Bosia, Arup AGU. Design team: Benjamin Aranda, Daniel Bosia, Chris Lasch, Ajay Manthripragada. Production team: Brian Belluomini, Meaghan Pierce-Delaney, Nick Desbiens, Toru Hasegawa, Sarah Herda, Jessica Lasch, Sydney Mainster, Molly McKnight, Elena Ossa, David Pysh, Jennifer Sabin, Wen Kai Tseng, Ricardo Vargas, Eun Jeong Wang, Jade Yang. Finalist, Young Architecture Program, MoMA/PS1, 2005.

We are indebted to the following people for their support:
Molly McKnight for her loving support and encouragement; Sarah Herda for being so true and so good for so long; our families Charles, Janice, and Jessica Lasch, and Arturo, Maria-Luz, Daniel, Doris, and Nicolas Aranda, for always being there; Anh Tuan Pham for making it all positive and inspiring; Cecil Balmond, Daniel Bosia, and the AGU for sharing great ideas and patiently educating us; Sanford Kwinter for shining lights through the fog; Detlef Mertins, David Ruy, Terence Riley, and Lindy Roy for being so supportive; Jane Harrison and David Turnbull for planting the seed; Bill Taylor for being a fellow traveler; Scott Tennent and everyone at Princeton Architectural Press; David Pysh, Dylan Pringle, Mark Wasuita, Daniela Fabricius, Jung-Ah Suh, Karen Marta, Joseph Grima, Matteo Poli, Christian Rattemeyer, Cay-Sophie Rabinowitz, Peter Hall, the whole Processing community, the Smart Geometry Group, Natalie Jeremijenko, Matt Scullin, Stephen Lynch and Jonathan Taylor, Kurt Lebeck, Jed Rothstein, Cristóbal Vicente, Sean Lees, Cynthia Davidson, Stephen Zacks, James and Mandy Wynn, Jorge Godoy, and Doug Diaz; and finally Steven Holl and Bill Stout for founding this great tradition which we are so honored to be a part of.

Pamphlet Architecture was initiated in 1977 as an independent vehicle to criticize, question, and exchange views. Each issue is assembled by an individual author/architect. For more information, Pamphlet proposals, or contributions, please write to: Pamphlet Architecture, c/o Princeton Architectural Press, 37 E. 7th Street, New York, NY 10003.

Pamphlets Published:

1.	Bridges	S. Holl	1977*
2.	10 California Houses	M. Mack	1978*
3.	Villa Prima Facie	L. Lerup	1978*
4.	Stairwells	L. Dimitriu	1979*
5.	The Alphabetical City	S. Holl	1980
6.	Einstein Tomb	L. Woods	1980*
7.	Bridge of Houses	S. Holl	1981*
8.	Planetary Architecture	Z. Hadid	1981*
9.	Rural and Urban House Types	S. Holl	1983
10.	Metafisica Della Architectura	A. Sartoris	1984*
11.	Hybrid Buildings	J. Fenton	1985
12.	Building; Machines	R. McCarter	1987
13.	Edge of a City	S. Holl	1991
14.	Mosquitoes	K. Kaplan, T. Krueger	1993
15.	War and Architecture	L. Woods	1993
16.	Architecture as a Translation of Music	E. Martin	1994
17.	Small Buildings	M. Cadwell	1996
19.	Reading Drawing Building	M. Silver	1996
20.	Seven Partly Underground Rooms	M. A. Ray	1997
21.	Situation Normal...	Lewis.Tsurumaki.Lewis	1998
22.	Other Plans	Michael Sorkin Studio	2001
23.	Move	J. S. Dickson	2002
24.	Some Among Them are Killers	D. Ross	2003
25.	Gravity	J. Cathcart, et. al.	2003
26.	13 Projects for the Sheridan Expressway	J. Solomon	2004
27.	Tooling	B. Aranda, C. Lasch	2006
28.	Augmented Landscapes	M. Smout, L. Allen	2007

*out of print, available only in the collection *Pamphlet Architecture 1-10*